To all those who thought they were alone. You're not.

I'M HERE!

3

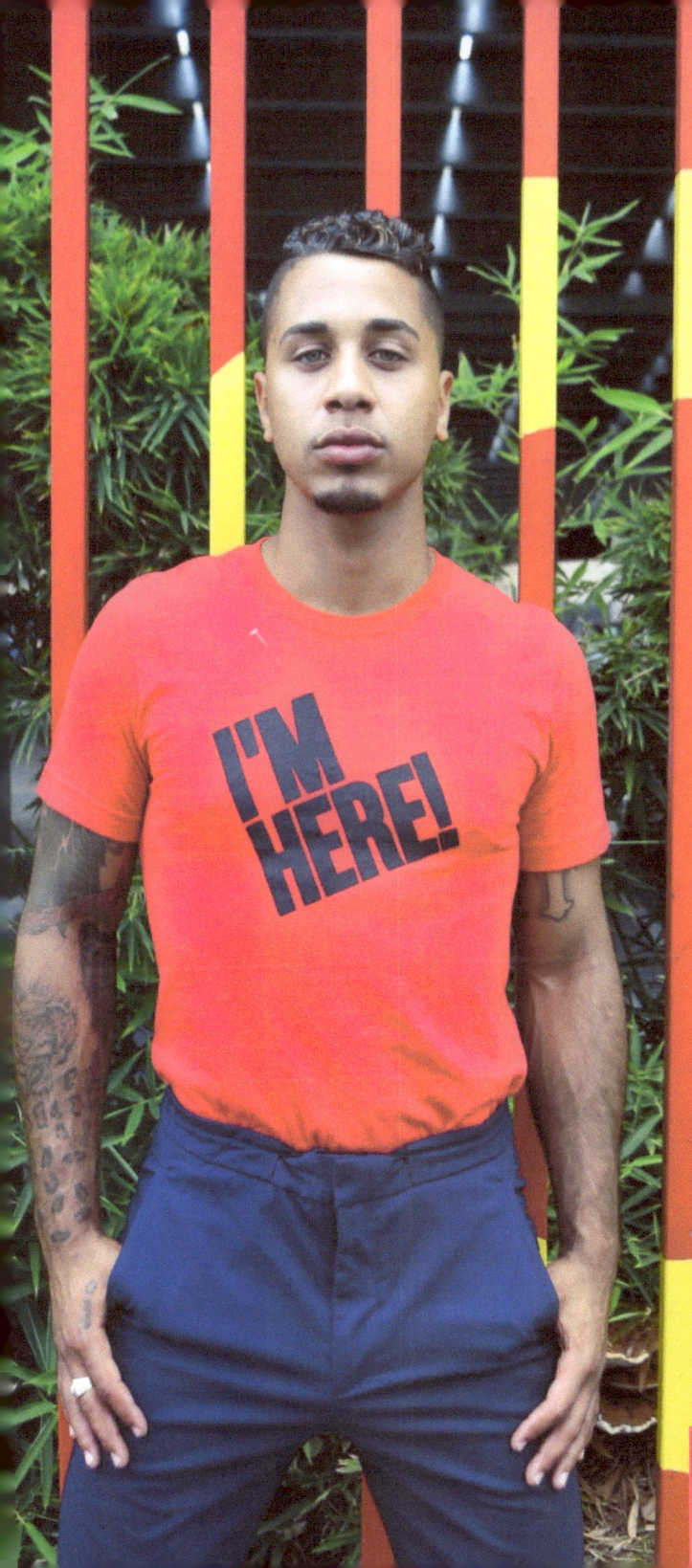

# INSPIRATION

*Never give up on something you truly love.*

*Life is like an amusement park: many rides, different obstacles, and open sunshine or rain. In the amusement park, you might get on a rocky ride, but that's just preparing you for the future – testing you to see how strong you are.*

*Don't ever give up on yourself or your dreams. Always Believe in GOD and yourself. Once you accept and believe IN yourself, nothing OUTside of you matters.*

*Always stay focused and be happy.*

*SMILE and enjoy LIFE !*

*#IMHERE*
*#BELIEVEINYOURSELF*
*#BEYOU*
*#DREAMBIG*

# TABLE OF CONTENTS

# ACKNOWLEDGEMENTS

First things first: Thank you God.

Thank you for always providing and answering my messages. Without you, as a child, I may have given up.

I would like to thank my mom. If it wasn't for you, I wouldn't be here today. I love for you that. I also want to say thank you for always believing and accepting me. I know we've been through hell and back, but you always said you were so proud of me. I love you. And don't worry, I never gave up on you either. You only have one MOM . I LOVE YOU!!!

Amani: you are my WORLD, my #1. You taught me so much in life. You were and remain always by my side. You've been there for me in my craziest moments. I lived more than half my life with you. Thank you for never giving up on me. Thank you for still being you and loving me when I let you down. I'm SORRY! I love you AMANI.

To my Auntie Michelle: you've taught me how to love. You taught me to think big and positive, to treat people how they should be treated - with love and care. You've always treated everyone and everything with respect and kindness; I admire that about you. You're my LIFE. Thank you for coming to my rescue as a child. I wouldn't have asked to be with anyone else. I love you Auntie — thank you

Thank you to my older sister Jessica. You've been my right hand since I was a kid, always there for me on my worst days, always listening when I needed a shoulder to cry on. You were there when I was getting beat, feeling my pain and knowing what I was going through. You are my secret. I love you and thank you.

Thank you to all MY REAL FRIENDS, my family and Supporters . Thanks for always believing in me. Thanks for pushing me to go further. Without a push from a friend, life can feel so hard and overwhelming. Thank you guys.

*Mrs Lynita Blackwell.* You've helped create this big moment in my life. I can't thank you enough for ALL the work done and patience shown me by you and your family. Just listening to your voice pushes me to strive to do better. Thank you for believing in me and my vision. Thank you for NEVER giving up on me. You've also treated and talked to me as one of your own. Thank you for listening and understanding my life. I could not have done it without you. Thank you for featuring me in your magazine, my first magazine feature, *BOLD Favor* March 2016. Thank you VERY MUCH for the opportunities you've given me.

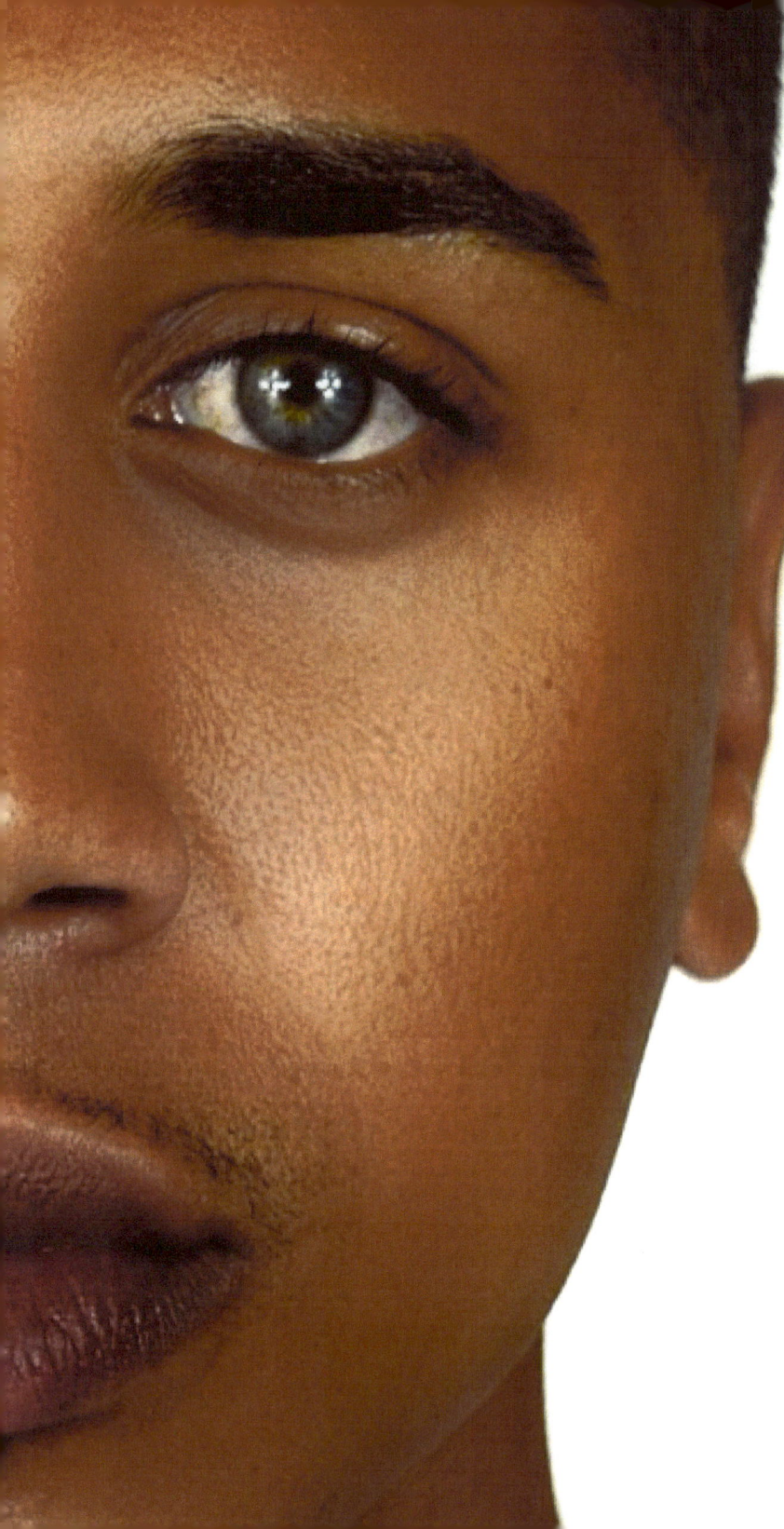

# Chapter 1
## How I Got Here

I was born Javonte Rosello, on October 26, 1992, in Manchester New Hampshire, Elliot Hospital. I was ready for the world, but my mom wasn't ready for me. Why? Because I didn't look like any of my family! My mom honestly thought I wasn't hers. When she looked at me, I was different: my blue eyes, wavy hair, and fair skin. Everything was different!

Different isn't always bad. It created in me a certain toughness to change. It was a good thing, too, because we moved around a lot. As a child, I remember always being in motion, at different houses and locations. I didn't know what was going on, but I learned to roll with it. I was blessed that my little sister was there to share some of the load, because some of the changes were really BIG.

There was this one time my little sister, my mom, and I went to the Dominican Republic. We were little, practically babies, the first time. It was an adventure meeting new people, experiencing new lands, feeling the DR sun on our faces; the spray of the ocean can't be described, only experienced.

The food was so good. Our relatives, there were SO MANY, were always hugging and kissing us, and telling us how pretty we were. I miss those times.

We went back and forth from the US to the DR a couple times before I started kindergarten. The last time before school started was rough. When I came back to the States, I knew something was very wrong, even at that young age. My mom was going through something bad, and all of us kids were separated.

The separation was HARD. I moved in with my Aunt, my sweet little sister stayed with my mom, my older sister moved in with my grandmother, my second oldest brother moved in with my uncle, and my oldest brother went with his grandmother. I really didn't understand what the heck was going on, why all of this shifting was happening, or when things would go back to normal. No one talks to you when you're little, they just expect you to "go with it". And I did, as best as I could, anyway. I learned pretty quickly that this was just the life we had, and we were just going to have to do what we had to do to live it.

Before you get too upset on my behalf, let me tell you what a blessing it was to live with my Aunt. Living with my Aunt was the best thing that could have happened to me. She was MOM, in every way. She was always there! It was like we were best friends and totally inseparable. I stayed with my Aunt for almost three years, until the summer after first grade. I'm so grateful that I began school surrounded by so much love, her love.

I was in Nashua, New Hampshire on Charlotte Avenue in 1999, and life was GRAND. I was very creative and my Aunt encouraged it. I loved coloring, I loved Pokemon, and I LOVED Arthur! I believe the first book I learned to read independently was *Arthur's TV Trouble*!

I don't remember this, but my Aunt said that I made friends very easily at school. (I'm glad because learning to make new friends, get along well with others, and being creative were the things that helped me build the I'm Here movement!) She also said that I did well in school and that I used to "always flaunt" myself. (That's totally believable because I love flaunting myself now! LOL) I loved to dance and still do now.

It's weird that my Aunt said that I was afraid of the Tooth Fairy; she said that I would always cry when I lost a tooth. (Who cries to get money? Me!) My first trip to the dentist came when I was six years old. I had my Adnoids removed, and threw up all over my Aunt. She didn't mind. She just hugged me tight and loved me, vomit and all.

Living with my Aunt was a fairytale. I felt like I went to sleep and one day woke up with the family I always wanted. Man, I was so happy!

One summer before second grade, I went back to the Dominican Republic and stayed for a couple months. I was a little older then, so I was able to communicate and understand a bit better what was going on. I almost wish I hadn't understood.

When I went back to the DR, my sweet baby sister went with me. But we didn't return together. I made it, but she didn't. My heart was broken! How did this happen?!

When it was time to return home, we didn't have any papers (documentation) as to our citizenship. (Remember, this was before September 11th, when airport security was a lot different than it is now.)

I was able to come back because I remembered my mom's name and information. But my sister was so small and I wasn't with her on the return. She didn't know any English, couldn't tell the security personnel our mom's name, or any other information that would help.

So I was shipped off alone back to the US. I felt like I'd left a piece of me behind. I knew I was going back to my beloved Aunt, but my little sweetie was there all alone. I know I was just a little kid, only seven, but I felt like I had let her down. I'll never forget the look in her deep soulful eyes as they pulled me away to leave. The memory brings tears to my eyes even now.

.

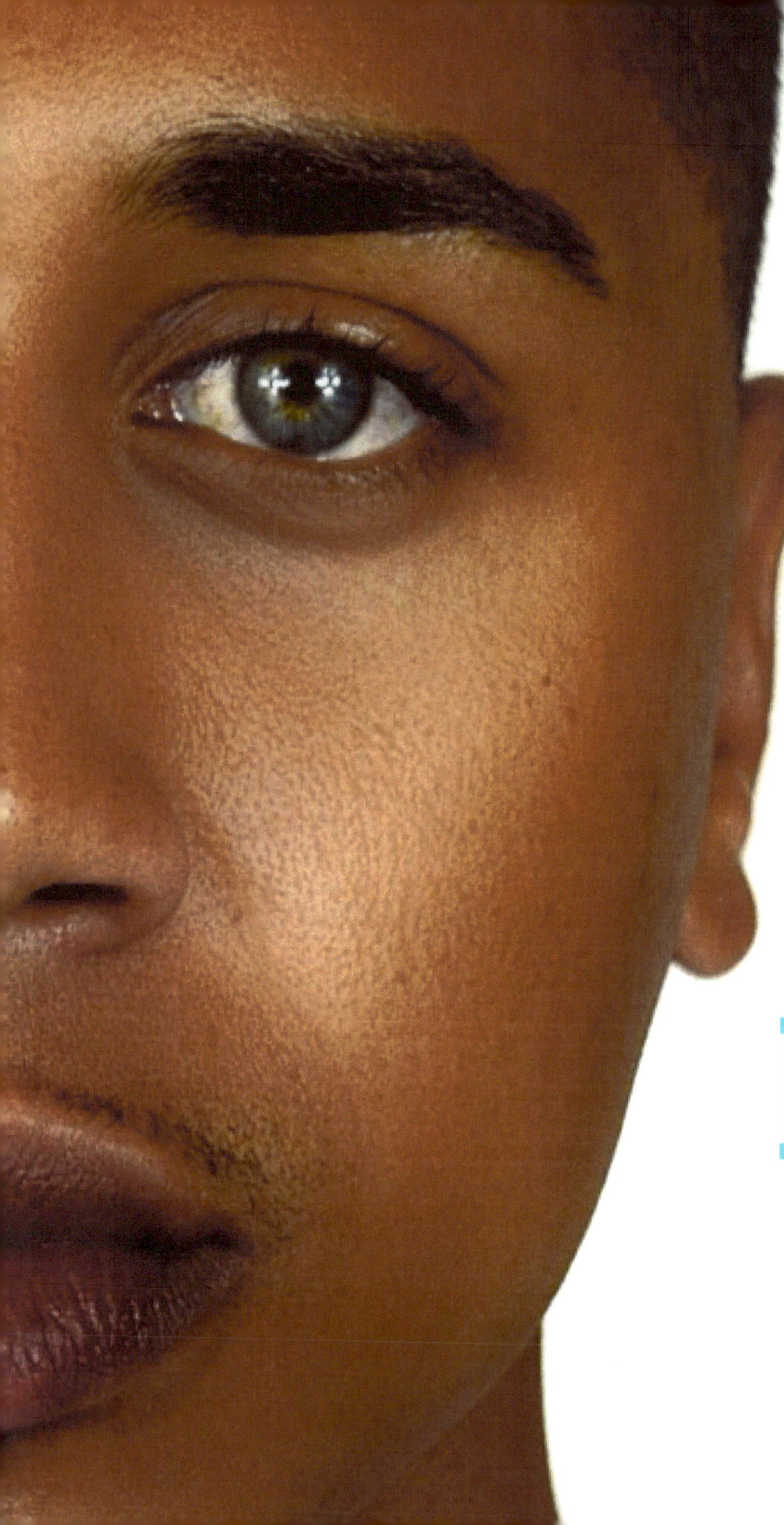

# Chapter 2
## My Family Is Here

I have a really big family. My mother had five kids: three boys (including me!) and two girls. Jason the oldest, Junior the second oldest boy, then me. Jessica was the oldest sister. She was like the mom when my mother wasn't around. We are still close to this day – that's my baby. Then my little one Jenieca. I swear we are twins in the afterlife. LOL

We are all blessed with good looks, and we all have strong personalities. I go back and forth about whether that's good or not. LOL

My siblings and I all have different fathers. It made life in the house pretty interesting, to say the least. Some of our dads were involved, some not so much. Looking back, I have a better understanding of how hard things must have been for my mom. There are people out there who probably think, "Why'd she have all of those kids if she couldn't take care of them?" Let me tell you, it's more complicated than that.

Love can make you do some of the craziest things!

My mom thought she loved our dads. They were good looking guys who talked good and had serious swag. When you love somebody, you try to create a family with them and a home. But then, you slowly realize that the picture you painted in your mind of how great that person is just is not real. That's what happened with my mom: when she realized that our dads were just regular guys, and that our dads realized that she was a regular girl, things fell apart.

It was really hard because things kept falling apart. I finally left home at age 16, but more on that later.

My mom loved all of us, but she didn't love us equally. It was especially hard for me because I've always felt and knew that I was different, and my actions showed it. I was different in a good way. I was brought up and learned how to talk and respect people at a young age. I knew then that I was going to be something big in life, and I didn't take no crap. LOL

Money was always tight, and my mom was always trying to "make a way out of no way". If there was some new hustle, she was going to try it. I can't tell you some of the things she did, because honestly, they weren't all legit; let's just say that I'm glad she never got caught.

I remember being so mad at her, especially once I had to leave my Aunt's house. I would think to myself, "Why can't you be like the other moms and dads?" But looking back, I better understood that she was just doing the best she could with what she had. The truth be told, I had it better than some of my friends at school. At least there were people like my Aunt and Grandma who did love me and told me how precious I was. Some of my friends were cursed at and talked down to by everybody in their families.

But I didn't realize that at the time because I was still going through a lot on my own. Adding to the drama of moving around a lot, and being shuffled from family member to family member, I was just trying to live my life and finish school. I know how hard it can be, believe me. When you feel like you have nobody, I mean seriously nobody, it can almost break you. And add to that feeling like there's no one to talk to about it and no one to look at and say, "Hey he's just like me," man, it hurts.

I, myself, felt that way at a young age. But something inside of me just always said NEVER give up. I want each and every one of you reading this to do the same. STAY STRONG and ALWAYS BELIEVE.

My brothers were really hard on me, calling me names, making fun of me, and calling me "soft". I learned not to let it bother me. But now that I say that, I realize that it never stopped bothering me; I just learned how to cope. You never learn how NOT to be bothered when people you love, and who are supposed to love you, treat you badly. You just learn to ignore them and pray that God removes you from the situation sooner rather than later.

The way I deal with challenges is to say to myself that this is just an obstacle, and it will be over soon. Anytime you're going through a situation, just remind yourself that there's always a stop at every obstacle, and that it's happening for a reason.

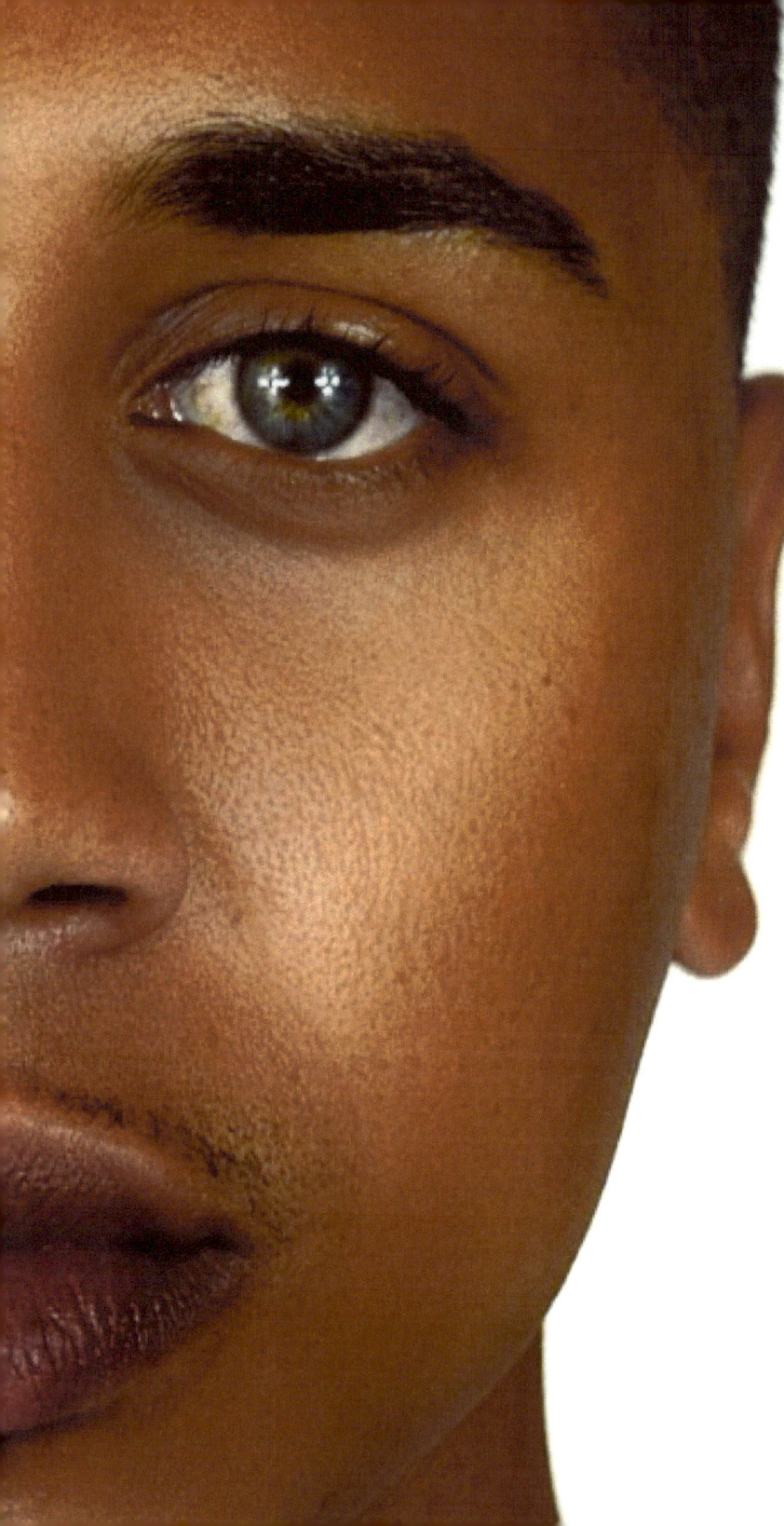

# Chapter 3
## Blame Was There

My mother struggled a lot. As kids, our focus was on ourselves. Even though we knew that something was off, we still focused more on trying to make things normal, or what we thought normal should have been.

There were times when we had to take care of ourselves as much as possible. Those cleaning-the-dishes days, OH BOYYY, were not my FAV. There were times when it would take us ALL day to clean the whole house. There was even a time when mom stopped cooking. Oh man, WHYY? LOL

Let me tell you: those siblings sure were used to momma's cooking. They couldn't cook a damn thing to save their lives! LOL

Thanks to my girlfriend at the time, Amani, we didn't starve. Amani started cooking very young. And who was right beside her, watching and learning? Yep, me! Man, she wanted me to leave her alone a lot, but I just couldn't because... I Fell in LOVE. Anyhow, we will get back to her later.

We were young kids, just trying to live life, but our efforts sometimes landed us into more trouble. I remember one time when my mom and us kids came home from the grocery store, my little sister dropped the milk and it spilled everywhere. Guess who got the blame? Yeah, me, and mom got me with the belt. As a child, I was blamed for a lot of things. I still to this day can't understand why. Well, hey, I still had to move on with life.

Looking back, I know in my adult mind that my mom was stressed to the max, and was doing all she could to hold things together. But in my child-like mind, all I could see and feel was anger, frustration, and incredible sadness. It was the sadness that bothered me the most. Her dealing with her situations and taking it out on us really hurt me. I think that's why I love the entertainment industry so much because it brings light and enjoyment to life, and allows you to create a new and happy world.

I've worked so hard in life to be able to do the things I've done and want to do, and am able to still be here today to make a change in other's lives. And the entertainment industry has made that possible.

I was born to help others, and it just puts a smile on my face to do it every day.

TEACHER COMMENTS

**FIRST QUARTER** Conference Date Nov 1999

**SECOND QUARTER** Javonte continues to struggle with issues of respect and authority. Although he is making slow, steady progress in all academic areas, often his behavior hampers his learning.

**THIRD QUARTER** Javonte is making strides in all areas—academic and emotional. He has a wonderful spirit for learning, enjoys the classroom and takes pride in his work. Great progress this quarter!

**FOURTH QUARTER** Javonte has developed a real interest in reading and writing. The progress has been incredible! He is eager to learn, but at times still struggles with self control. He will enjoy 2nd grade.

Promoted To Grade 2 Room

**HAVE A SAFE SUMMER!**

# Chapter 4
## How I Got Here

God, I love my grandma! I call her "Memere" (pronounced "muh mare"). Being hugged by Memere is like being wrapped up in sunshine. I swear, that woman radiates love. When I have my family, I'm going to love my kids and grandkids just like that.

Memere was the best cook, and her house was always full: full of people, food, and parties. Man, did we party! She loves her family. She knows how to talk to people, makes everyone feel like they're the most important person in the world, without making other people feel left out.

Memere also doesn't take crap from anybody! Her house stays clean, and if you don't want her to tell you off, you'd better keep it clean! LOL

I mentioned that we moved around a lot. But one thing was certain, Memere knew where all her kids and grandkids were, all the time. She didn't play that crap. She wasn't able to keep all of us because of her health and money being tight. But she made sure that we were fed, clothed, and went to school, no matter whose house we stayed at.

And I remember some of the good old times my Uncle Belcourt would come over and do some funny acts and skits. He would have EVERYONE cracking up. He did one called the BABY STEPS. Man, he was so talented! He would have everyone laughing!

I think my love for my Auntie and Memere led to my desire to love others and make them feel special... and despite all the crazy ish (and there was plenty!), my childhood days were pretty awesome. Because in addition to my family, there was Brieanna.

This girl went everywhere with me: we stuck together like glue from second to ninth grade or so. We still talk to this day. She treated me like a bonus brother, and more.

As I was growing up, I came to believe that my feelings towards girls were getting stronger. I met Amani, my first girlfriend. We would always "make up to break up", and everybody in town knew about us. We were THE POWER COUPLE. When we had our break-ups, I dated other girls in the town. Amani would always be mad, but she couldn't let me go.

Amani's mother, April, was always there for me growing up. She was like my mom. When me and my mom would get into arguments, she would come to the rescue.

Amani was really cool. She still is to this day, and to eternity, will be my NUMBER 1.

11/6/05

This is my favoritest
Aunt in the world I
love her so much
she's like my mom!
and she treats me
good and like I am
her son!

Aunti Michelle

23

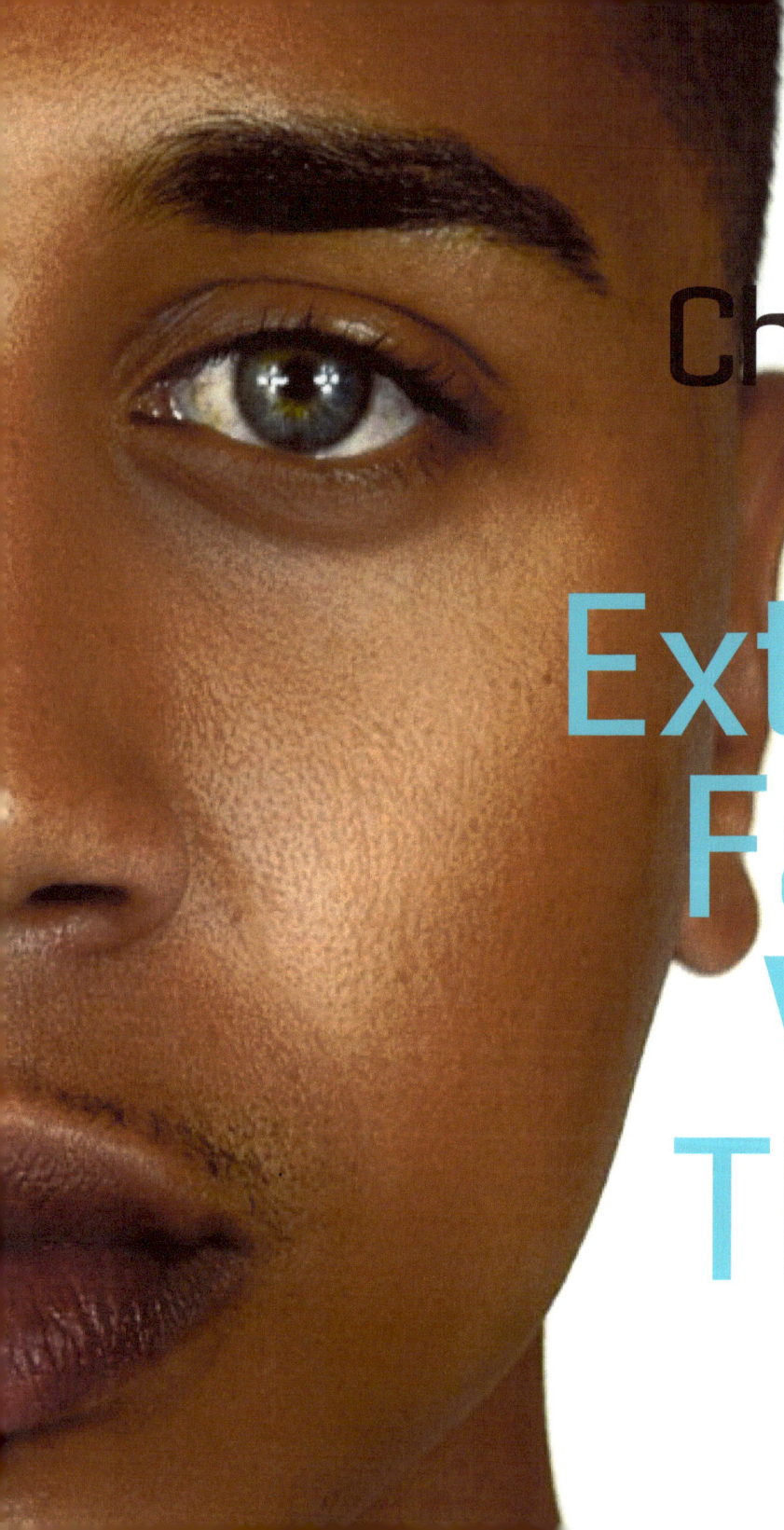

# Chapter 5
# My Extended Family Was THERE!

God always provides — in every way.

There were times I thought I wasn't going to make it. Growing up is already hard, even if you have the perfect TV family. You go through all those changes mentally, emotionally, and, don't get me started on the physical! (I was always fine as wine, LOL, just kidding!) Seriously, when you're trying to figure out who you are and people are constantly asking you, "So, what do you want to be when you grow up?" All you can think to yourself is, "How the hell am I supposed to know? I'm trying to figure out who I am TODAY!" Man, it gets to be a bit much.

You already know my life was far from perfect. All the moving around made it hard to feel at peace with the world. Then, feeling like you belong to a different family because you're so different from them is sometimes scary.

But God provided.

He gave me an amazing extended family that has loved me and supported me. When I moved on to Boston, I was so thankful for Alexandra, Danna, and Luis. We were road dogs. And boy, let's not forget about the man that brought everything to light, Hector. Hector was my older brother, uncle, friend and mentor. He's shown me a way in life as no one has before. He introduced me to this family and they let me into their home.

During my times living in Boston, I met more A M A Z I N G people: Cassie, Geni and Janisa. Boy, oh boy, what wonderful times we had. Cassie and I were thick as thieves and were always hitting them parties. Her parents were amazing and accepting people, and had an open heart.

Geni was a BITCH at first. UGHHH, she was so mean to me back then. We were always fighting. I think she low-key had something for me, and was upset because I dated her best friend. LOL Over the years, we became brother and sister. I would NEVER trade her for the world (but maybe for some Jamaican FOOD though! LOL).

Janisa AKA JLO: this women right here, is my TIGHT. We go back before I moved to Boston. She's the sister, friend, mother that you tell ALL your secrets, and she saves them.

Cassie, Geni, Janisa and I were the Four Musketeers! It still amazes me to this day how we just clicked. It was like pieces of a puzzle coming together. And God knows I needed that.

Jenieccaget's what
she wan't more
than me I can't
live like this god
please please help
me. I need it before
something happends
more the worse
then it is!
welig2g

♡ Scwonte

P.S GOD
HEIP ME
PIEASE

I
Love
GOD

27

# Chapter 6
# Feeling Lost and Having No One THERE

I had my Auntie there to stabilize things during early elementary school. But by the time I hit middle and high school, my life had gone off the rails.

I lived with my mom, and she was doing any and everything she could to make ends meet. Looking back, I can't imagine how scared and alone she must have felt. Even though our family, her mom and siblings, pitched in when they could, they were all struggling, too. So there was only so much they could do.

Because my mom was so stressed out, she took a lot of her frustrations about the world out on us, especially me. I think I was too different for her. Not just the way I looked, but the way I acted, too. She came to accept that I was different, but my dreams of acting and modeling were a bit out there. She wanted and needed me to do something that brought in money NOW and was reliable.

It was hard for me as a kid having dreams and thinking sometimes they wouldn't come alive because of what I was going through. I tried to help where I could. I started little jobs very young. I'd cut the neighbor's lawn, and shovel the snow in the winter time to buy clothes and other necessities. I wanted to help my mom, but I also needed to save so I could head off to New York to pursue my dreams.

I eventually got there, too. Man, them NYC days: me and Jaide, my girlfriend over 11 years, used to do everything together. We did house parties and ran the NYC streets. But back to that later!

Me trying to save my money to get to NYC caused so many fights with my mom. She wanted the money, and I felt that it was mine because I had earned it. Obviously, she didn't agree.

There was this one time when our fight got serious. She hit me and I started screaming at her, calling her names. She got that belt and I took off running. We were chasing each other like mice after cheese. I ran out the house and didn't come back for a few days to let her cool off. Looking back, I wish I had given her the money in some situations, but I don't beat myself up about it because in my child's mind, I worked hard for my little dollars.

Thankfully, I had my friends, and they were there for me. I had a place to stay whenever things got beyond heated at home. I had someone to talk to when I was overwhelmed. I had a place to wash my clothes when I was on my own at 16. It was my extended family, my friends, who had my back.

11/5/05

Today was a good day at first! Me and Jenieca went to the mall together we both bought a Build bear, I got a girl and I named her Novemba she's brown with nice hair! Jenieca got a boy, he's oh! But when we got home I hated it! I hate everyone in this exept Jenieca, Sometimes, Then Junior calls me names and all that stuff and I don't like it, but when ever I try to tell my mom, she tells him 2 stop but he dont and I HATE Vicky 2!
well by

♡Javonte

11/6/05

Today was not a good day 4 me, cause all I did was get yelled at, I do not like anyone in this house, all my mom does is call me names and I hate that I just want to run away so bad! right now I am in my room crying to death I can't live like this anymore! she calls me prick and everything I hate it so bad but what could I do about it though she treats me good sometimes but alot of times she dont

31

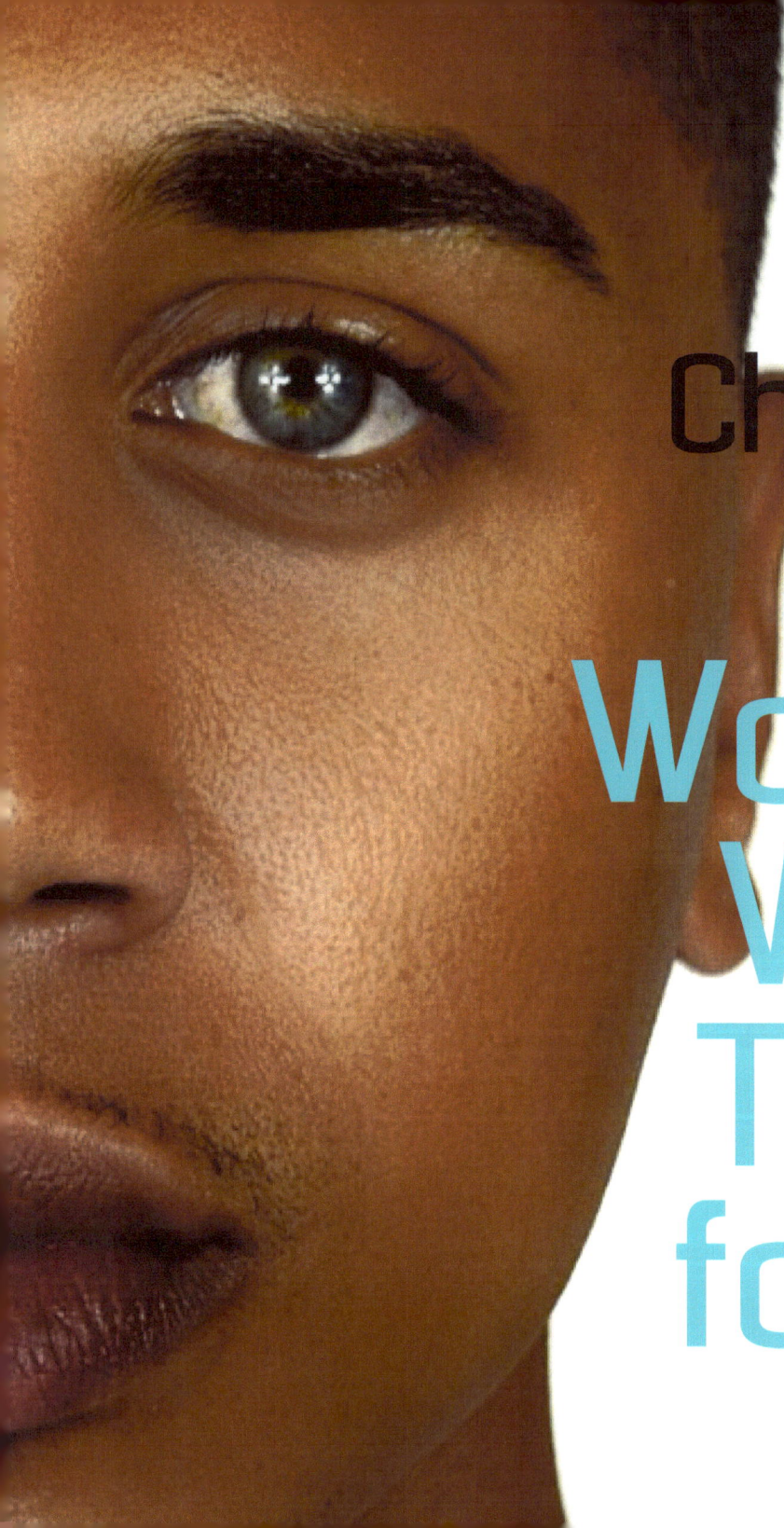

# Chapter 7
# New Wonders Were There for Me

Life is truly wonderful, full of wonder, if you give it a chance.

Second and third grade were full of wonder for me.  Although there was a lot of movement, I went to Beach Street Elementary for second and a portion of third grade, and finished third grade at McDonough Elementary. My child's heart was able to appreciate the beauty of life. I realized early that music and dance took away my pain

I remember a time around Christmas, actually Christmas Eve, we (the kids in the family) were allowed to open one gift. I had asked for a CD player and some CD's. I got JaRule, Ashanti and Beyoncé. I was so happy! I went to my room and listened to Ja's melodic flow, Ashanti's sweet siren's call, and Beyoncé's sultry soul all night. I was in heaven and never wanted to leave.

But I did for my hamsters!  My favorite animals in the whole wide world were hamsters when I was young. My sister, Jenieca, and I played with our hamsters all the time. Jenieca had a girl and I had a boy. One day while we were playing, we noticed the girl was acting weird. We suspected that she was pregnant, but couldn't be sure. We were only little kids, what did we know, right! LOL

Well, the next morning, we woke up early for school and heard noises coming from the cage. We went to go check and guess what? Jenieca and I became aunt and uncle!  The girl hamster had been pregnant, and there were her babies, six in all!  All those baby hamsters were squirming around and the mama had one in her mouth as she was feeding it. I was in love! I was an uncle — and a daddy! The cage was full of little babies running around.

I thank God for those happy moments with my music and my

hamsters because they made the other parts of my early elementary years bearable, along with my friends, Brieana and Esther.

Brieana was always down and riding for me. We used to have so much fun at recess, and played in the park across the street from the school. Esther was just my twin and we all did everything together.

I also loved dancing, and kept that going for a long time.

Although I loved my school Beach Elementary, I hated the fact that there was always lice going around. Thank goodness I was a boy, and my hair was short, so I didn't get lice. But I remember my friends always having it and not being able to play because they had to be kept from everybody else.

I also hated being bullied. I remember one time, I believe it was third grade, I got into a fight in the back alley because some boy had called me gay and bad names. It was after school, so nobody caught us, but my friend saw us and broke it up.

We were always moving from one house to another and from school to school. So by the time things started getting bad at Beach, I moved on to McDonaugh. It was there that I fell in love with basketball! Man, I loved that game. I loved moving down the court with the swiftness of a cheetah, and pretending I was Kobe Bryant laying up those three pointers. Looking back, I can say objectively that I wasn't very good, but I had heart and loved the game.

So I tried out for the team. I remember like it was yesterday! I went into the gym, confident and nervous, all at the same time. I did all the drills and everything else they asked us to do. I was so tired, but it felt good. The next day, I came to school, dying to see who made the team. They posted the list on the wall, and we could see everyone who had made it. I looked down at the bottom and I couldn't believe it – I MADE IT!!! I was so happy, my heart was beating so fast, but then I noticed an asterisk next to my name. It said-wait for it-the WATERBOY! They'd put me on the team all right, as the waterboy! I was so mad! But I was on the team, right? And maybe I could prove myself if I worked really hard.

So I tried it. I went to practice, came early, stayed late, worked hard, didn't talk back, and did exactly what was asked of me. But inside, I was still steaming. I could only hold myself together a couple of days before I quit. I just couldn't take it. In those brief moments that I thought I'd made the squad, I'd told anybody who'd listen that I was going to play! It was too much for me to go to practice, watching the other kids do what I wanted to do, and then have to serve them. I know that it would have been an opportunity to learn and grow, but remember, I was a little kid in the fourth grade.

I didn't have to suffer the embarrassment for too long because I transferred to Bakersville Elementary during fourth grade and stayed there through the fifth. We'd moved AGAIN — this time to Welch Avenue. That's when things really started to change.

I was diagnosed with Attention Deficit Hyperactivity Disorder (ADHD) and was prescribed medication until 5th grade. My mother made me take it, but my older brother and aunt didn't want me to because it changed my personality. Also, they didn't believe I needed it. They realized that my inattention in school was more to do with us moving around so much as a family. (Newsflash: dysfunction has an impact on your mood!) That was part of it.

Well, fifth grade came and I stopped seeing the nurse and no more medication! But there was something else that affected my mood, something no one knew. I fell in love.

35

Javonte Rosello

Her name was Amani. (Yes, the same Amani from before.) OMG, I was SO infatuated with her! We used to see each other a couple of times a week at the Boys and Girls Club. When we were together, the world fell away. All I wanted was to be with her. We dated from that point on through high school...

# Chapter 8

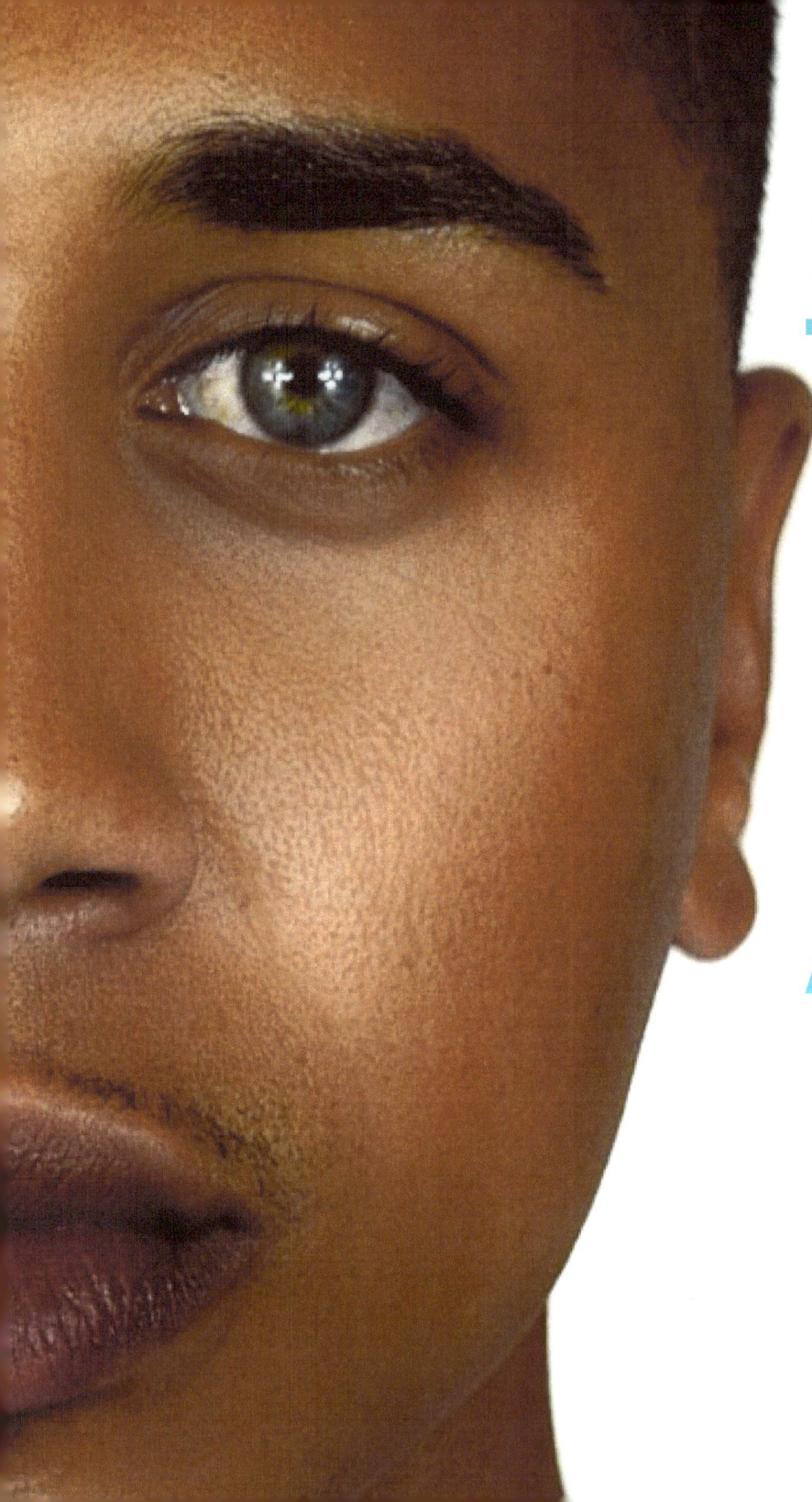

# The DR Was and Always Is There

The Dominican Republic was an experience. The last time I was there, I was a teenager. I was about 15 and half years old. I withdrew myself from school, I believe it was during the 10th grade, and went to the DR.

I was having a hard time at home, dealing with relationship problems with my mom and other family members. I just wanted to get away! I wanted a new life, so I looked to my dad's side of the family and started speaking to them. I remembered the love and connectedness I felt while I was there as a small child, and wanted to feel that again. I NEEDED to feel that again desperately.

I built up a pretty good relationship with my dad's side of the family, and then one day I was off to the DR! I had been working odd jobs and saving money for quite some time. I used my savings to buy a plane ticket to my new home and my new life.

Walking off the plane, I was a bit nervous. It was really humid and hot out that evening, but it smelled so good. I could smell the ocean and the sun.  And the breeze made the hair on my arms stand up.

And then it happened. I met him. I met the man my mother had loved and lost so many years ago. My dad. I met my dad for the first time.

He picked me up from the airport.  When he walked up to me, I was shaking.  He hugged me tight, and I hugged him right back.  We didn't speak for a long time.  Then we walked to the car and drove away.  It was a long ride, but a short ride.  It was long because it took an hour to get to the house from the airport. But it was short because I was finally with my dad and I didn't want anything, not time, space, nor anything else, to get in my way!!!!

As we drove to the house, I remember looking out the window. I saw the differences between how the US and the DR operate, and how different the environment and life was out there. A lot of homes were on hills. There were big open fields with nothing in them. There were lots of cows and horses just living free. Life sure was different coming from America.

I was surprised to learn that my dad owned a car rental spot. We went there because my dad lived in the back. This is where we stayed. It was quite different for me coming from a big house with my own bed and lots of clothes to an empty room in a rental car place. But I was game. I was with my dad in the DR!

My dad was actually cool for the first couple of months. He would take me all around to see the family, and show me off to his friends. We visited all of the DR (or that was how it felt! LOL).

I learned a lot about my dad in a short amount of time. He was a hardworking man. After serving time in prison, my dad was committed to turning his life around. He was very dedicated to his work and his family. On my dad's side, he had three kids that I knew of. When I saw them, they remembered me from when I was a child. There are two boys, and one transgender woman.

Now you'd think that my sister being transgender, and I being interested in guys before knowing my status, you'd think he would be accepting and supportive. NO NO NOO!

It took him a while to cope.

My dad, and in my experience many Dominican fathers, are VERY much against gay people. He wasn't accepting of my transgender sister, and I did not tell him I liked guys. I had already come out to the world back in the US, mostly because I realized who I was so young in life. But when I moved to the DR, I didn't tell anyone. I already knew the situation. Life over there was different. The dads didn't like their sons wearing earrings, wearing "feminine colors", tight clothes, or walking with a "swish". They didn't like any sort of the "gay look".

Before I relocated to the DR, we had so many fashion trends, and I rocked them on the island. At that time, it was all about skinny jeans, colored retro jeans, and extensions. It was a very fun and outgoing time. I brought those trends with me to the DR, and they looked at me like I was crazy. LOL I had to explain to them that this is how we dressed in the US.

Eventually, after months had passed, and I was living free, riding on the back of my brother's motorcycle, things came to an end in the DR. My dad just turned. I guess he was upset because I didn't have his last name. WOW, things got crazy. My mom didn't have money at the time to help me out. It was a bit of a struggle, but boy, I lived and learned.

So here's what happened: I had to get in touch with my sister's side of the family, and I spoke with my aunt. She came to the rescue, and I stayed with her for a few months.

I got back to the US because of the kindness of a stranger named Roberto. I'd friended him on Facebook. I didn't know it at the time, but I had dated his husband. (I did not know the guy was married when we met, but once I realized it, I broke it off with him.)

Roberto sent me a friend request and I accepted it. We became cool and he purchased my plane ticket home. Now, I tell this story nice and neat, but BOY OH BOY, that was a mess!

I still to this day don't understand why my Dad was so upset about me not having his last name. But as there was so much shit I'd already been through, I didn't look back to find out. I went back to the USA and started a new life.

Dear Javonte , hope you have a fun birthday party. When I'm at your house you make me happy all the time. From Janine and Jordan

THE REPORT CARD

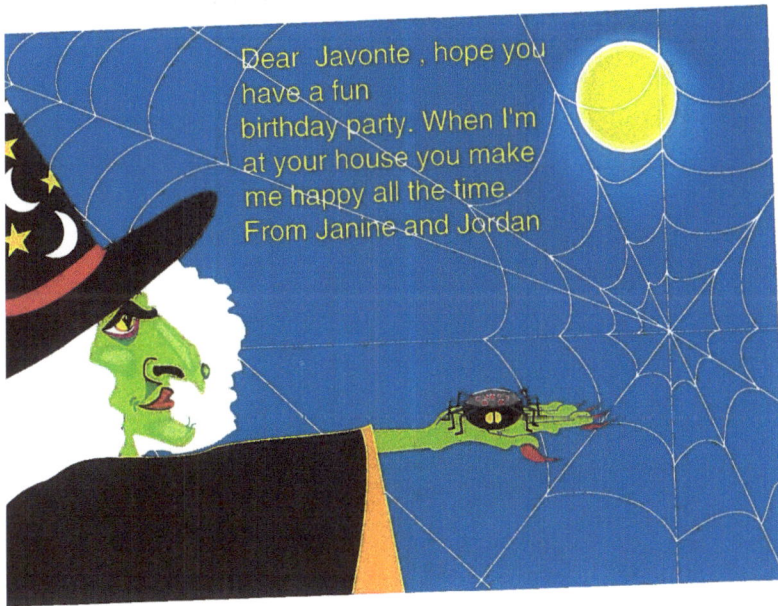

progress and a source of future goals.  It is essential that good communication card envelope and you will be contacted.  Progress will be discussed at a parent

**SYMBOLS**

Important goals and skills for each learning area are listed and student progress is indicated as follows:

C - Commendable          S - Satisfactory
I - Improving             N - Needs Improvement
M - If this student's instructional program has been modified from grade level
    expectations, this is indicated beside Reading, Writing, and/or Mathematics

**TEACHER COMMENTS**

FIRST QUARTER    Conference Date Nov 1999

SECOND QUARTER  Javonte continues to struggle with issues of respect and authority. Although he is making slow, steady progress in all academic areas, often his behavior hampers his learning.

THIRD QUARTER  Javonte is making strides in all areas — academic and emotional. He has a wonderful spirit for learning, enjoys the classroom and takes pride in his work. Great progress this quarter! ☺

FOURTH QUARTER  Javonte has developed a real interest in reading and writing. The progress has been incredible! He is eager to learn, but at times still struggles with self control. He Promoted To Grade ____ 2 ____ Room will enjoy 2nd grade. ☺

HAVE A SAFE SUMMER!

43

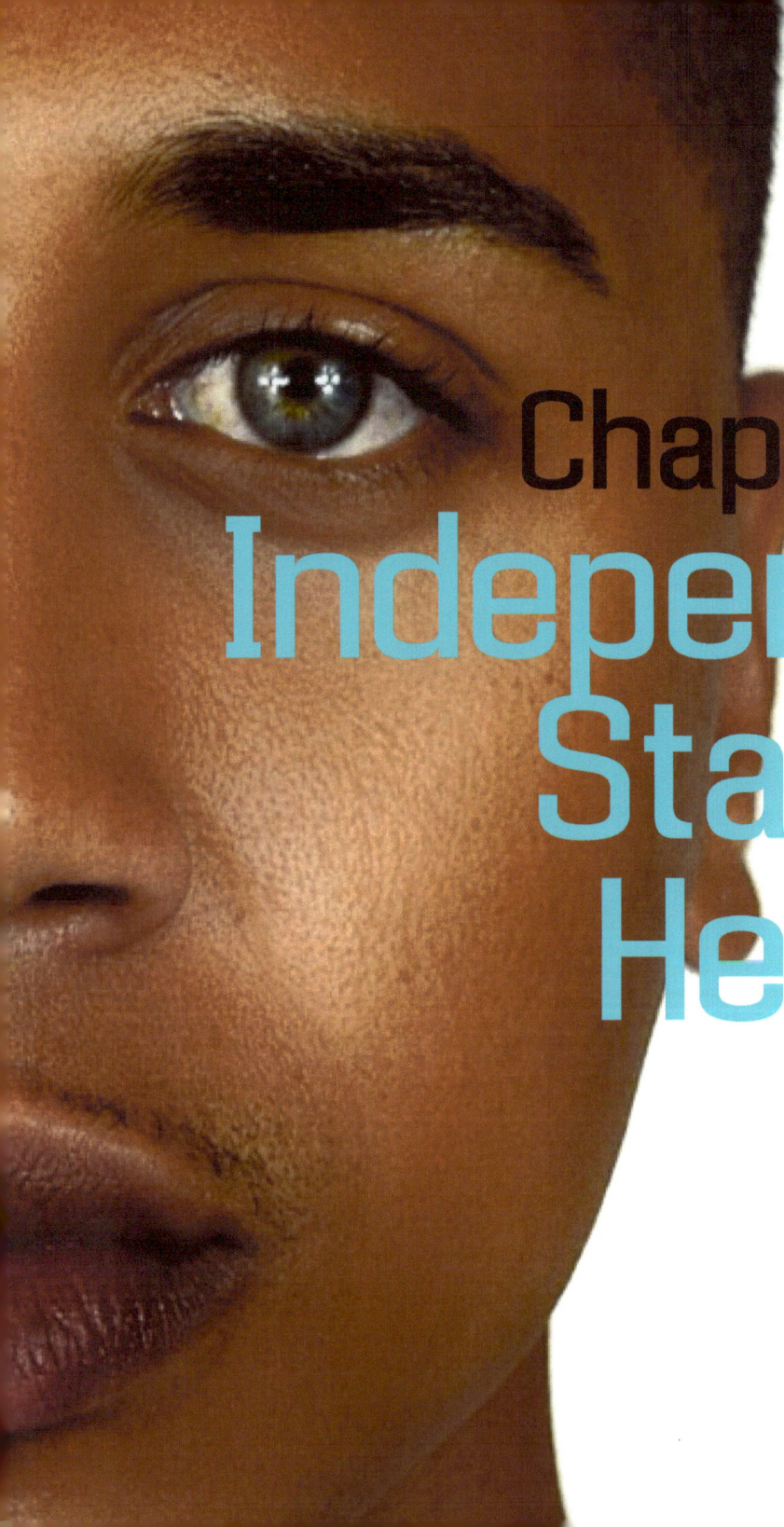

# Chapter 9
## Independence Starts Here

When I moved back to the USA from the Dominican Republic, I was 16 years old. I came back to my mom's house, and re-signed myself back into school.

After living in another country for a year, I now saw the world, and everyone in it, very differently. Living with my dad, and out of the country, created in me an independence and appreciation for money management and responsibility that served me well in high school. And I still use those skills today in managing my business interests and the I'M HERE movement.

I am so grateful for my years at Memorial High School. Those four years were like walking into freedom. I had longer days at school, wonderful teachers, and good friends. I did, however, stop talking to a lot of people because I felt that they were the ones causing me not to focus. That year out of the country made me get my shit together.

Molly was one of my best friends in high school. I became very close to her and her family. They understood what I was going through at home. They let me in with open arms.

I remember this one time we tried to throw a big party downstairs in her basement. Her mom made some cheese and hot dog things. EVERYONE in the room cleared; it smelled SOOOO bad. It was too funny. We had some really good memories.

I made friends with the upperclassmen easily because everyone knew Junior (my nickname), and probably because of my life experiences in the DR. So, I didn't have a problem with anyone picking on me.

There were a few kids who called me gay here and there. But after a certain point, I just didn't pay those people any attention. I'd been called gay since elementary school and through my teens. So by high school, that crap went in one ear and out the other. I had too much going on at home, and dealing with the normal school crunch, to really pay attention to those idiots.

I joined the dance team for a couple of years. Dancing was my passion and a way of expressing my anger. Even though things were going well at school most times, I was still a teenager with a lot of emotions rolling around within me.

Dancing helped me process those feelings. And, of course, my music helped, too! I remember I went to my first concert to see Sean Paul. He was my favorite artist back in the day. Oh MAN, those lines were so LONG, but hell, it was worth the wait.

**Strawberries**
MUSIC & VIDEO

TICKET SALES

PALLADIUM, THE
WORCESTER
CHRIS BROWN

04/13/2006 THR
07:00 PM Door
GENERAL ADMISSION                    25.00
  ALL AGES                            4.25
00000000000043330166939
  SERVICE CHARGE                     29.25
                                     29.25
  TOTAL
  CASH

ALL TICKET SALES ARE NONREFUNDABLE

4/7/04,

Dear Journal,
Today was an ok day
I went to school and then
came home I was
just hanging around
with amani at her house
then Dagi called us and
asked if we wand to
go to the Manchester
Wolves game, so we said
yeah and got dressed
was me, Jose, Amani, and
Dagi, and some other white
boy, we all went then
Amani diched us for
Greg and them, me and
Amani got into an
agrument and the she
walked home by her
self and she was
mad at me then I →
walked home! Good Night

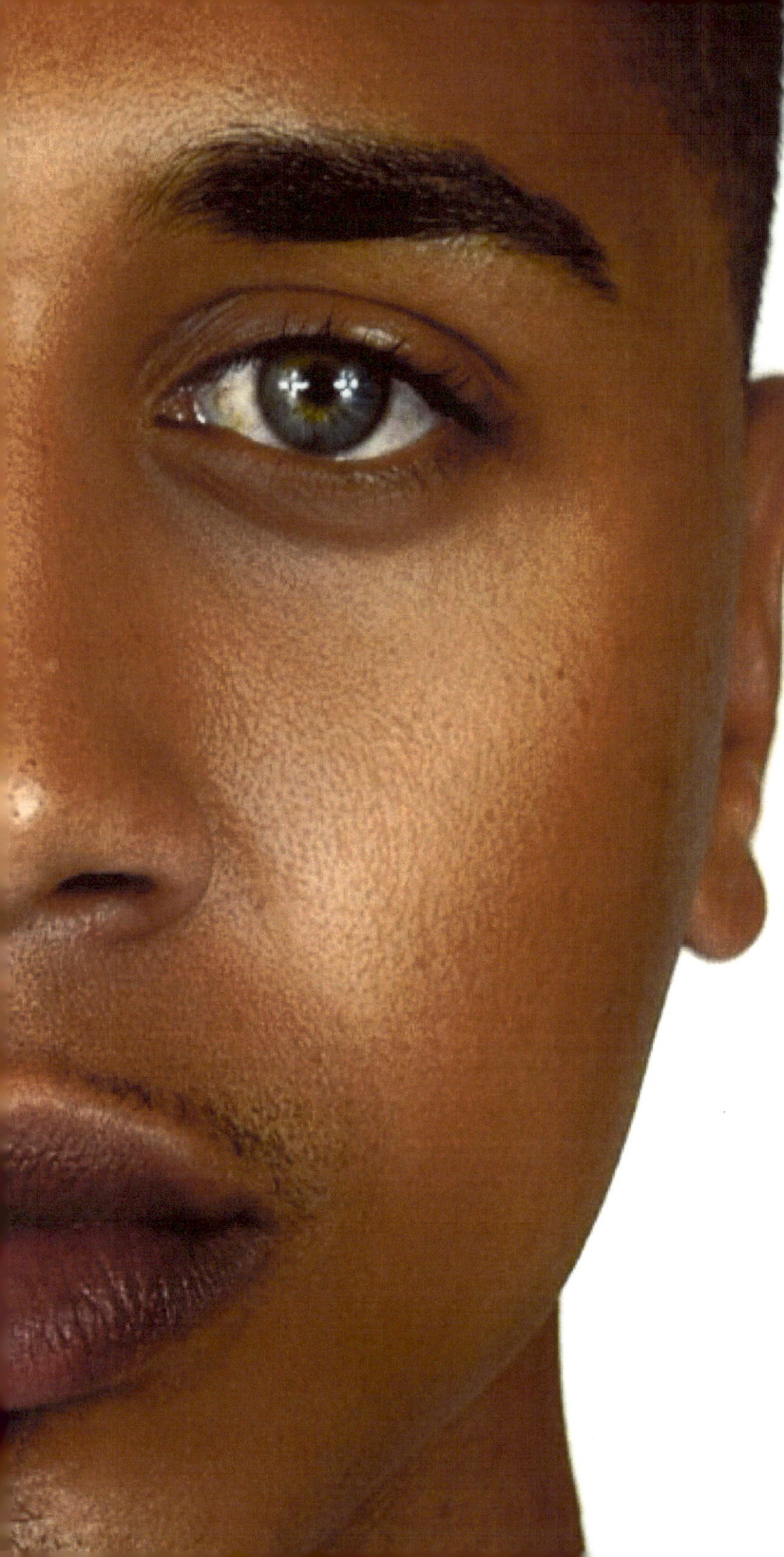

# Chapter 10
## Bullying Started Here

Being Bullied at home started young for me. I remember my youngest and second oldest brothers would always pick on me, calling me gay, and sometimes stabbed me in the back of my head with pens. My mom wouldn't do anything about it, other than to tell me to stop crying.

Being bullied at home is worse than being bullied at school or at work. Home is supposed to be an oasis, a safe place from all the drama and craziness in the world. Unfortunately, that wasn't the case for me. People at school were much more supportive than the people at home in the early years. They'd always pick on me because I was small and couldn't fight back. (It's sad that we play "kick the cat" when we're hurting instead of dealing with our own pain.) I forgive them for hurting me, but it still makes me sad when I think about those times.

In addition to my brothers picking on me, calling me names, such as "gay boy", "big lip Jamaican", and "prick", sometimes my mother would tell us that she wished she'd never had us. I wish it was just name calling, but there was physical abuse as well.  Things were rough on both ends.

I hated it when my mom said, "I'm on my way." It meant that she was going to beat me. I was a normal kid, and got into mischief, but some of those beatings were uncalled for and unnecessarily brutal. I suffered and cried my nights away. I felt like the child called "It". There were so many times I prayed and asked God to please give me a new family. It didn't happen. But what He did do was make me strong and resilient. I learned to always keep my head high and to smile through it all. I didn't fake it like everything was okay, but I realized that I was going to have to be my own hero and rescue myself from the situation.

So when I got old enough to work around the neighborhood earning some money, I did. It was how I was able to finally buy a plane ticket to the DR when I was 15.

I was so fortunate, blessed really, that my Aunt made me feel like somebody at such an early age. She made me see life in a different way and to think differently. It's how I forged the determination to never give up.

Guys, I know that there are times when you feel like you want to end it all, or, to stop and just sit down. I know we all do. Just remember: you were placed on this earth for a REASON; so you live that reason and stay STRONG.

I believed in myself since a young age and knew that I was going to go far. My mindset was just different, and it was that thinking that made me different from my family. But that difference in thought birthed my freedom. That was the day I became free. I felt like a bird that was let out its cage - free.

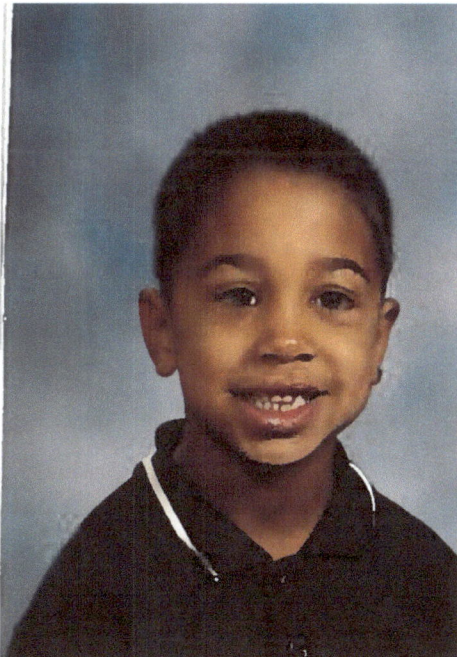

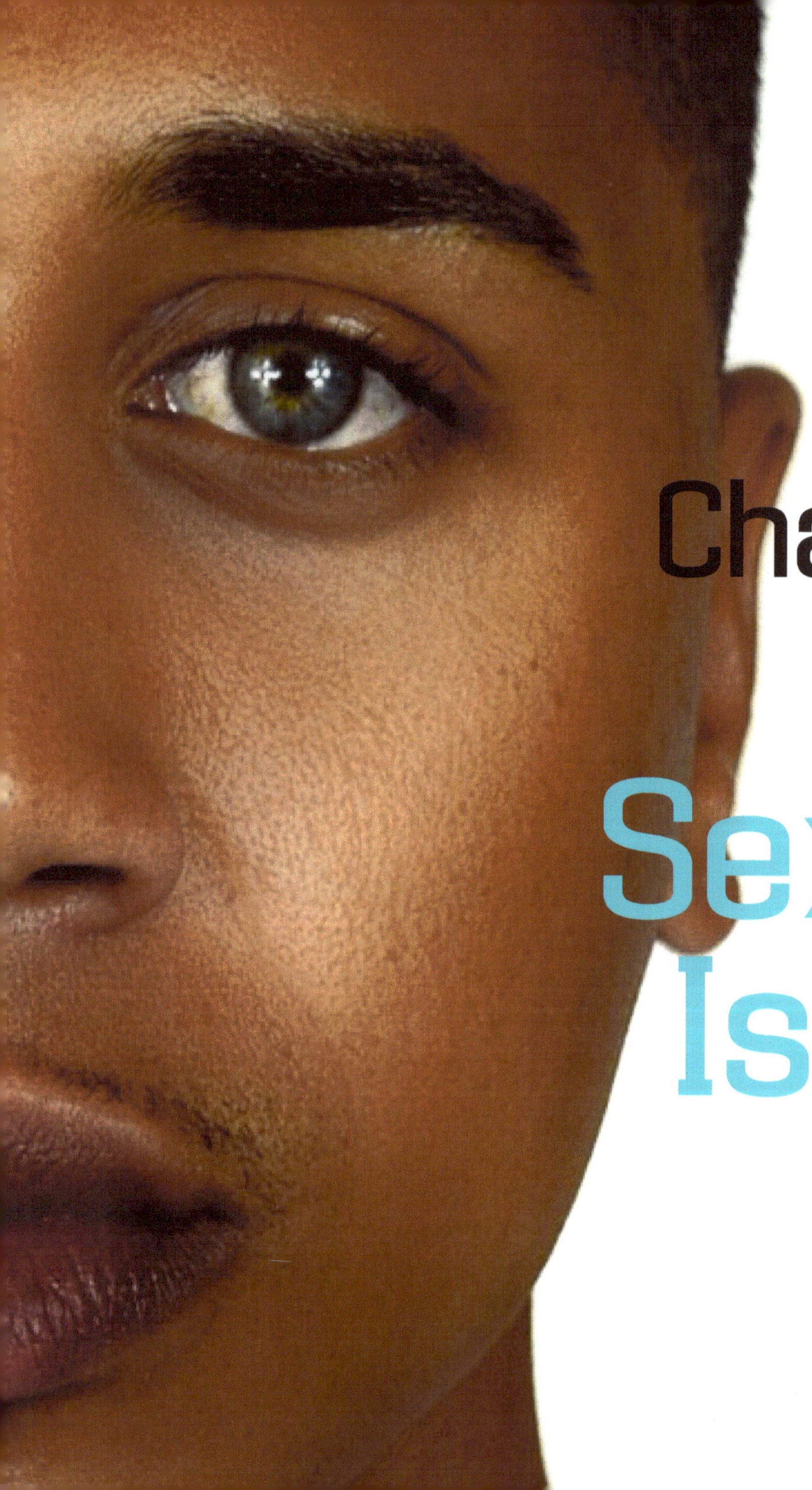

# Chapter 11
# My Sexuality Is Here

My awareness of sex and my sexuality started very young. When I was a child, I remember being in the Dominican Republic and my older brother and cousins touching me, and playing with each other's private parts

I grew up from there.

I remember one time when I was in Boston in the winter. I asked my father to take me to my friend's house to hang out. I stayed the night, which was a surprise. My dad didn't usually like me staying over at people's homes who weren't my family.

My dad didn't know that the guy I was hanging out with was a guy I was hooking up with. Remember, I kept my sexuality from my dad.

The next day I left and went back home. The guy and I were "talking", as we used to call it. We were boyfriends. I felt liberated and was tired of living under the radar. So I came out Jan 1st, New Year's Day.

I wasn't afraid or nervous; I just felt like myself, regular. It's no wonder, that apparently, I'd gotten drunk the night before and told everybody at the New Year's Eve Party that I was bi-sexual. That's how my mom found out; someone at the party called and told her. She called me the next day and asked me if it was true. I told her yes. She didn't hesitate. She told me she loved me for who I was. Being gay or liking a man didn't affect the love she and my family had for me.

It was a real turning point in our relationship.

Things weren't perfect, and didn't get better overnight. But the fact that my mom was there for me at such a tender time really made a huge difference. I'll love her forever for that.

But, of course, this story is bittersweet: the next day, the boy I'd been talking to broke up with me – over the phone! I was so embarrassed. I'd just posted our pictures all over MySpace! But I got over it quickly, and just went along with my life.

But SHIT if I had known, I'd have stayed with Amani! LOL

Gratefully, I still had all my friends around me to comfort me, and life from there just went on...Or so I thought. I started feeling some kinda way, so I hit it to Jaide's house in NYC to reflect. And then it hit me.

DAMN, I felt bad. REALLY bad. I found out that Amani saw the pics on MySpace and that her life fell apart when she saw me posted up with that guy. You have to understand, Amani NEVER cried, and there she was crying *on her mom's shoulder*.

I crumbled. That was my babe, my number one, my everything. Although I liked guys, I still LOVED her. We got back together, somewhat after that, but it was never the same.

5/3/05
This book belongs
Please do not
read beond this
point on!
11:15AM
Scorpio
180
6th
Southside

# Chapter 12
## Gotta Get Outta Here

Once I fully embraced who I was, I didn't realize it then, but I was emancipated. I was truly ready to be an adult and take care of myself.

I remember the last time I lived with my mom. It was the middle of November in my junior year. I had been working at CVS for a few months, but was hiding my job from my mother because she would have tried to take my money. She found out I was working, but not where. She was pissed that I wouldn't tell her.

After battling with her for some time, I finally got my mom to back off. But I had to agree to watch my younger sister after school. That meant letting my sister in to the back room of the store where I worked when my mom wasn't able to watch her after school.

One evening I forgot to go home and let my sister in the house. She was locked out the house for a little bit. It was dark and cold. I was next door with Amani.

When my mom got home and saw my sister outside, she called me and told me to come home. As soon as I came through the door, all hell broke loose. My mom started screaming at me. She took my keys away, grabbed me and pulled me inside. She and her boyfriend shoved me around the house, then finally pushed me inside my room. She took out the light bulb, took my bed apart, and removed my mattress. My mom told me I had to sleep on the floor before locking me in the room by myself.

I remember just being stuck in that room for hours crying and just felt tired. I knew I had to do something. This was the end of it, all of it, for me. I pulled out my phone; I'd bought it with my own money. She'd tried taking that from me, too, but I wasn't having that! I called my girl, Amani, and we came up with our Master Plan.

I had Amani go to the bank and take out all my money from my account. I knew it was a matter of time before my mom saw how much I had stashed away. My bank statement came to the house, and she used to intercept my mail and open it. That always made me so mad!

Amani went off and did it. While she was on our mission, I waited until everyone fell asleep. Once I was sure everyone was knocked out, I went to the kitchen and got a few garbage bags. I packed everything I wanted and needed to make a new life for myself. I had about six bags full of clothes and shoes.

I got a set of curtains and a bed sheet, tied them together, and hung each bag, one by one, out the third floor window. As each one fell to the ground, Amani grabbed them and hid them in her car. I got the rest of what I needed, and ran out the back door. I never looked back and never lived with either of my parents again.

I was on the run for a couple of weeks. My mom called my phone from random numbers, trying to find out where I was. She found out where I was working, I'm not sure how, on December 3 of that year, and came down to the store. She made a huge scene, yelling and cursing me out. It was at that point that my manager found out the situation with me and my mom. I had to let him in on everything, which made me even madder, because I was such a private person.

Once my manager knew the entire story, he had my mom escorted out of the store. A few minutes later, I was asked to leave my job so that I could go home and attend to her.

I went home with my mom and her boyfriend. I was very upset; I didn't even want to look at her. I was so embarrassed!  I kept thinking, *You coming to my job and making a scene like that!*

I walked up stairs, and my mom started hitting me and yelling at me. Her boyfriend was talking shit too.  Then cornered me in the living room, told me I had to sit on the sofa, and they wouldn't let me get up.

About 45 minutes passed, and my mom's boyfriend went to work. That left just the two of us and my sister, Jenieca. I got up to go into my room, but my mom grabbed my sweater and pulled me toward her. She yelled at me and dragged me into the living room.  She was already strong, and her rage made her even stronger.  I was trying to get away without hurting her because I didn't want to make things worse.

She finally released me, but it was so she could swing at me.  I ran toward the door, but she was closer and made it before me. My mom closed the door, then called my sister to help her keep me there. They both tackled me and held me down. She once again locked me in, this time in my sister's room. She sat inside so I wouldn't get out.

We argued and yelled at each other through the door, and she called me all sorts of names.  She then told me she was going to call the police because she "just can't take it". And she did it.

They asked her what happened. And, oh my God, I still can't believe and will never forget what she said. She told them that I hit her.  She told them that I scratched her arm, and that I had put her in a headlock.  I couldn't believe the words that came out of her mouth.

The officers came and they questioned each of us. At the end of the day, it didn't matter that I denied everything. They took me in "the wagon". I didn't and still don't fully understand why a parent would ever do that to her child. I was in shock. But it didn't take me long to come out of it. And when I did, I fought back!

I got myself an attorney, and fought the charges against me. I got a restraining order on my mom so that she couldn't ever force me to come back to her house. Our extended family found out about it, and I asked my grandma to take me in. She lived about 45 minutes away. Thankfully, I'd saved enough money to buy a car, and had purchased it a few days before all of this happened.

I used the car to go to work and to school. No matter how bad things got, I knew that I needed to finish high school. Sometimes it'd take me over an hour to get to school because of the distance, but I didn't give up. It was the middle of winter, and the weather was terrible. But I kept on.

Unfortunately, (or fortunately, I'm still not sure which one) the school found out that I was living outside of the district, and told me I had to move closer. My brother and his family lived down the road from my school. I stayed with them for a little over a year. Life with them wasn't too bad. I got to have my own room and a little more freedom. They made sure I paid a bill and had some responsibilities. And I got to play with their sweet little baby boy. Also, staying with them allowed me to graduate school six months early.

That was when I was able to move to Boston and start my new life.

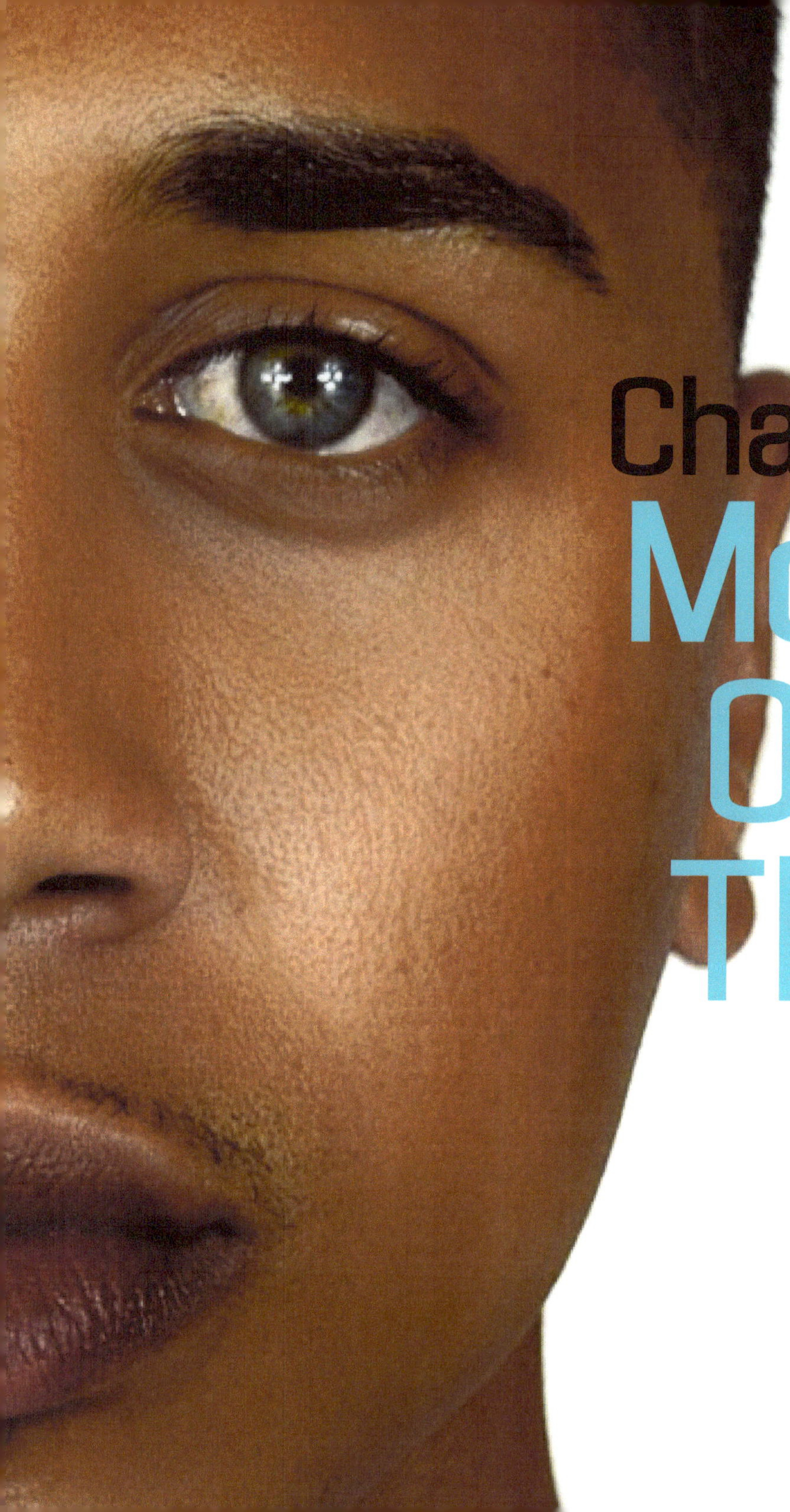

# Chapter 13
# Moving On to There

I moved to Boston right before my 18th birthday. I was out of a job for a couple of months, but I had saved some money from CVS before moving.

I was really blessed to find good people from the start. I had met this wonderful and loving family through a really good friend. I became a part of this family. I was very close to the daughter, Danna. She was like one of my own sisters. The little boy was a pain at first, but he became like a little brother to me, and I gave him anything he asked for.

Alexandra was the mom. She was amazing! She knew everything that was going on back home. I told her the story, unedited. We came to an agreement: I'd help her out with bills and food in the house, and I could stay as long as I needed. I went out every day looking for jobs, day to night. Eventually, I got a job at Panera Bread. I started working there for a couple of weeks. Then I got a call from a bank. I interviewed and got the job. Then another job called, and it was a position to open up the first Smoothie King in Boston, on Newbury Street. I worked all three jobs at one time. I was all about my work, and going to the gym during my free time. I had to work a lot to save for what I wanted and to pay bills.

After a couple of months at the bank, I quit the other two jobs and stayed with the bank. Deciding to quit the other two jobs was easy. I knew that the bank was where the next great thing in my life was going to come.

See, the first day I walked into that bank on Cambridge Street, I had not ever been so nervous and scared in my life. I'd wanted to work at a bank for a long time. So when it happened, I didn't want to mess anything up.

When I had interviewed at the bank, I had butterflies. You know the kind you get when you want something really bad to happen? I didn't feel that way when I got the other jobs. And also, the lady who interviewed me took my breath away. She was about four feet tall, the cutest person I had ever seen. Her name was Sharon. Sharon had such a bright smile and the most beautiful personality. She was kind, but no nonsense. One thing I can say, she didn't play about her job! She interviewed me and a couple days later she called, and I got the job. From that point on and to this day, we've been stuck like glue.

Sharon was one of my go-to's. We became really, really close; people at the bank started getting jealous.

Then came Christa; me and this lady clicked as soon as we met. She has an amazing heart and soul. She's like my older sister, mom, and best friend. We told each other things that no one ever knew. I thank this woman for everything she has done. She's made me a brighter and stronger man. She was my manager and sister at the same time. During those bank days we took hours for lunch. They couldn't tell us what to do! LOL I'll always be there for this woman.

Working at the bank gave me a sense of power and authority, things I'd never felt before. I gained a sense of confidence and worldliness that matured me fast. It was the most professional job I'd ever had, and I took it seriously. My co-workers became my family.

# Chapter 14
## Getting Out There

I've always been into modeling and taking photos. My modeling career really kicked off when I moved to Boston at age 17. Once I officially was on my own and was able to go to casting calls by myself, I did that as much as I could.

When I was younger, I always needed a parent with me, and I didn't have that consistently. I remember one time my sister brought me to an event in Boston while I lived in New Hampshire. But she wasn't able to do it as frequently as was going to be necessary for me to make modeling and acting my full time gig.

So I got really serious: working hard at the bank, working hard at the gym, and going to auditions and casting calls.

I was really fortunate to have embraced social media early. I started off with MySpace at about 14 or 15. Back then, that was the place to be. This was before Facebook, Instagram, etc. I loved taking pictures of myself. (I know, SURPRISE! LOL) And so I did lots of photoshoots, and posted them online. The pictures were great. I was and am very blessed to work with excellent photographers. They helped me gain my following and establish my name "The Blue Rose". One thing I learned from that experience: people always remember your face, then your name.

I worked MySpace before and while I lived in the DR. Once I got back to the US, Facebook was the thing. My friend, Roberto, brought me back to the US and helped me to establish myself on that platform. Thank you, Roberto. I don't even know where I would be if not for you.

Then came Instagram. People saw my pictures and started sharing and reposting them. As my following grew, my name was floated about the modeling industry. My stature was really getting big! I was and am so grateful to God. Things were finally going my way after so much pain!

I was able to learn the in's and out's of IG, which was good for me. So as time went by, I would Shout Out people (SFS) — and I learned that by doing a couple of those, I gained those people's followers.

As my name began to expand, I started working on my brand. I always wanted to have something of me to leave behind that was unique and special, something that would help and make people feel really good about themselves. I wanted to establish an EMPIRE, that would be a brand of clothing, wonderful photos, positivity, truly provide a voice for others who needed it, and a helping hand.

So I got to work. I was able to use my IG platforms for my name and brand. As I posted other people's hash tags, they hash tagged everything about my picture and shared it. I gained followers and likes. Those wonderful people became my customers and my tribe.

I was always myself; no fake shit here. I'd been through too much to try to be somebody I wasn't just to sell some items or get followers.

Once you can accept yourself and believe in yourself, you don't give a damn what other people have to say.

People saw me being myself, always posting positive content, and just living free. They would ask me all sorts of questions, like how I could be myself so comfortably, how I got into the modeling world, and how I stayed so positive. And I responded for real. People appreciate REAL people.

# Chapter 15
## I'M HERE

As I started feeling comfortable with myself, I shared my story. Some people were really surprised because they couldn't believe I was so positive after all I'd been through.  A lot of those people who came to know the story helped me, blessed me, and supported me.

I'd been receiving messages on social media for a while at that point, telling me that I was a wonderful model, and that they looked up to me. But then, late summer 2015, young kids started reaching out to me, and telling me their problems. I'm no counselor or therapist, but I have my life experiences. So I responded with that. I told those kids to stay strong. I told them that life is a roller coaster and soon, you're going to get off. I told them that I'd been in their shoes, and that sometimes life feels like a nightmare you will never wake from. I told them to keep their heads high and believe in themselves.

These kids were 14, 15, 16 years old. They were going through problems at home. They were being picked on at school.  They weren't being accepted just because they were different.  I told them people are always going to have something to say.

You have to learn how to ignore them, stand tall, head high, and just keep                                                                      walking.

I never tried to make it seem like I had all the answers. I don't. I never told them that I knew EXACTLY how they felt, that I could imagine based on my experience, but I didn't and don't know for sure.  And I never told them that I could make things all better because I couldn't and can't.

But what I COULD do was be there for them.

So I'd just say, "I'm here."  And I was.

The first time I ever said, "I'M HERE!", a light just popped in my head. It just opened another path in life. When I answered those messages, it felt good inside. I felt accomplished. I was helping people get through their situations. Nobody truly knows EXACTLY what you've been through, but they can understand. I understood.

Some can relate and some just care. It feels good to know that there are people in the world who care and show support for you, sometimes more than people you've known forever. I am that person.

My goal is to give people who've been mistreated and bullied a voice and a different, more positive way of seeing life. When people who are going through situations see someone around their age who made it through a similar situation, it gives them hope. It gives them life. A part of them feels good, like they're alive and being seen for the beautiful people they truly are.

I'm going to keep giving out positive energy, just believing in myself, spreading the word, and showing people that bullying is NOT acceptable or allowed in any way!

I realized that I needed to make some money to fund my movement. So I started my own brand two months later in October 2015 called THE BLU ROZE. I chose that name because it is my last name and my eyes are blue. Once my tee shirts and wristbands started gaining popularity and selling, I started my first line of tee shirts called IM HERE! I wanted to come out with something BOLD, something strong that had a powerful meaning. IM HERE! was it. I knew with the right movement and the right people it could go far.

I was living in Charlotte, North Carolina at the time, so I gathered a few people off Instagram who lived in the city.  They are so amazingly supportive!  I had two girls and one other boy: Jasmine, Jessica, and Shakur.

It was December 19, 2015, and I directed my first photoshoot for IM HERE! I started out with black and white shirts. We wore funny glasses. We played around with different props and poses; we were very creative. Thanks to the genius himself – Ty the photographer – magic was created.

I posted our pictures on my social media pages and started to advertise the shirts. People really liked them! I was so happy, and I was energized!  A few months later, I came out with BLU ROZE tee shirts and phone cases. The business was going really well and I ALWAYS let everyone know how much I appreciated their support.

I worked on nothing else for two months straight.  I was up all day and night searching for and trying to get more information and help to keep growing. It took me a while to get it all together. There was a point where I felt that I'd asked a lot of people for help, but no one seemed to respond to me. But that didn't make me give up.  Starting my company was something I'd always wanted to do. So I kept going!

I opened the store January 26, 2016. I got my first two orders that same day. I was excited!!! It showed me that people really DID care and supported the movement.

I kept searching for other brands I could work with to share our message.  I was looking on Instagram one day and passed by @BOLDfavormagazine. I scrolled down at some photos. I checked out the website and looked up their information. I saw that they were a magazine that "highlights Bold people, organizations, and causes". I emailed the owner Lynita Mitchell-Blackwell, and shared my story with her. She got back to me within a week or so, and she loved it. She said she would love to feature me in the March 2016 issue. I was so thrilled! It was my first magazine appearance ever!

From there, I just kept posting my photos, tee shirts, other items to advertise my company, and the IM HERE! movement. I got an email from an event that was happening in Atlanta in April, and I did my first fashion show with IM HERE! I shot my first video for IM HERE! in Los Angeles that May. Then I collaborated with Mrs. Sonji Willingham and her company Premeire Transitional Services. During that time, we (Lynita, Sonji, and I) worked together to create a new website and social media pages for IM HERE! And then had my first speaking engagement June 24, 2016 at Auburn University, thanks to Ms. Sonji. I am SO GRATEFUL to her!

Things went so well in LA that I decided to relocate there. My acting and modeling careers really took off. I have been featured in some videos and catalogs, and made some great connections for I'M HERE!

# Chapter 16
## My Journey Is Here

I am so incredibly blessed. My life has truly been an amazing journey, and I thank God for it every day, even the rough parts. Because of these experiences — good and bad — I'm able to help other people.

When I decided to relocate to Los Angeles, I packed up my belongings and business, and started afresh in a new city I'd never lived before. Thankfully, the same skills that helped me make new friends quickly while in school served me well in LA.

Being in LA really helped me to grow and to heal. I was finally living my dream and able to see clearly what my family members and especially my mom was going through so long ago. It enabled me to reconcile with my mom, and we got to the place where we were talking almost everyday. It was great!

I am so very grateful that I was able to reconcile with my mom when I did because she passed May 2017. Before she died, she told me how proud she was of me, and that she was sorry for all the things that had passed between us. I really respected the fact that she never made any excuses or tried to make it seem that her actions were justified. She owned her shit, and said that she was sorry. And that was good enough for me.

I miss her so much. Her death was so sudden! One day we were on the phone talking about the great things coming up for the IM HERE Movement and my business, then the next day I'm getting a call from my sister saying mom is dead. It hurts so bad to write that sentence. Mom is dead. I still can't believe it.

But I'm still here. And I'm doing the work I know I was meant to do. My mom is now a Guardian Angel watching over me, and is ready to kick anybody's butt who messes with her Blu Rose!  LOL

I'M HERE!

Fin.

Javonte Rosello is the founder and CEO of the anti-bullying and young people's empowerment movement "I'M HERE". Author of the breathtakingly raw biography "Behind the Blue Eyes: I'm Here", model, and actor, Javonte is a multi-faceted professional who works to incorporate his talents to empower people world-wide.

# ABOUT THE AUTHOR

Javonte's life has taken many turns. Growing up, he was bullied about his looks, his style, and his overall demeanor. Where some young people find respite at home, that was not the case with Javonte: he had a very difficult relationship with his mother that led to his being homeless at 15. Since the age of 16, Javonte has worked to support himself and in spite of the enormity of his circumstances, graduated from high school six months early at 17. A very grateful and humble person, Javonte credits his success to the warmth of good friends and his faith. "I knew God was with me, and I vowed to never give up because I knew He heard – and hears – my prayers."

While working as a banker, Javonte focused his attention to refining his acting and modeling skills, which has led to prime shoots with designers Amber Rose and Danny Miami. He utilized social media to promote his profile, and started a blog detailing his life's challenges. Young people from all over the world reached out, asking Javonte how he maintained such a positive outlook on life after being bullied and abandoned. Javonte responded to each message, giving hope and inspiration to keep pushing forward, that life really would get better. And he always ended each message saying that he was there for them. That message – "I'm here" – resonated within Javonte so strongly that he knew what he had to do: build the organization and infrastructure to bring more people into the fold, to let them know they were not alone, and that there were many people who were there for them. That was the birth of "I'm Here" anti-bullying and youth empowerment movement.

"I'm Here" has garnered support across the USA, and soon it will be international. Featured in several magazines and blogs, "I'M HERE" is growing in influence due to the simplicity of its powerful message and the stylish apparel bearing the brand, available at www.thebluroze.com.

Javonte currently resides in Los Angeles, CA. Follow the movement on Instagram at @imhere.4u. To bring Javonte to your organization for an empowering and motivating experience, contact him at www.imhere4u.org.

www.ingramcontent.com/pod-product-compliance
Lightning Source LLC
Chambersburg PA
CBHW061047090426
42740CB00002B/63

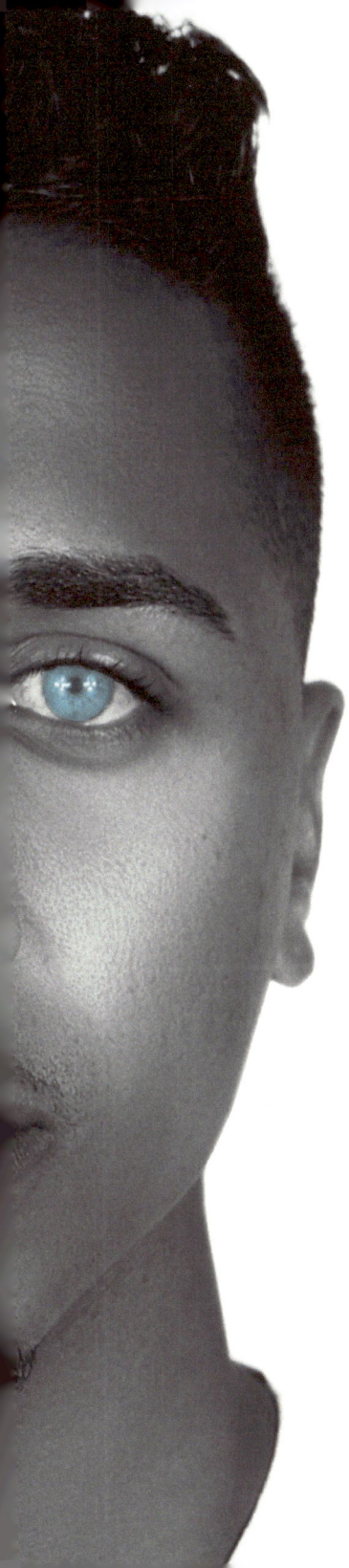

# BEHIND THE BLUE EYES I'M HERE

JAVONTE ROSELLO

For Information, Contact:
Leading Through Living Community, LLC
6790 Broad Street Suite 300
Douglasville, GA 30134

ISBN-13: 978-1-949266-01-6  Paperback
ISBN-13:  978-1-949266-02-3  Ebook